LOOK AT YOUR BOSS!

REHABILITATION FOR YOUR CAREER

Look At Your Boss!

Acknowledgements

Over the past year since I originally published this book, I have found my connection to God and all He has done for me has increased. I thank God for the words of wisdom and the Blessings bestowed upon my life and my family. I thank God for putting me in the position to move people forward.

My Wife Jeannett is my major and minor support system. She has sacrificed her life to allow me to pursue my dreams in my career. I love her with all my heart and I am thankful that God has blessed me with such a wonderful woman.

My Children
Lemar, Janelle, Sasha, Malcolm, Jenae

My Parents
James & Theresa
John & Patricia

My Siblings
Kim, Sabrina, Louis, Todd, Malik
Precola, Donna, Tondia, Jr.

Coney Island Cathedral Family
Bishop Waylyn Hobbs Jr.

Core Church Family
Senior Pastor Tim McCarn

Air Force Family

ITT Technical Institute Family

Jaime Hope for sharing her story

Special Thanks to Curtis Hoag
For cover design and photos

Look At Your Boss!

Look At Your Boss!

About the Author

James Sutton Jr. is the former Campus Director of ITT Technical Institute in Charlotte, N.C. He is a 'life learner' who has received numerous educational degrees. He loves to motivate and encourage people to succeed. James is an Elder at Core Church in Mount Holly, NC.

James is a 23 year retired United States Air Force veteran. He has received numerous awards with his highest honor being 'The Airman's Medal' for Bravery.

James has over 20 years' experience in Recruitment, Management and Personal Development.

His credentials include: Two Associate of Applied Science degrees from the Community College of the Air Force in Human Resource and Aircraft Maintenance Technology; a Bachelor of Science degree from Southern Christian University in Ministry/Bible; a Master of Science in Management from Liberty University, and is completing a Master of Science in Information Technology from Strayer University and concurrently pursuing a PhD from Northcentral University.

A native of Brooklyn, NY, James is the husband of Jeannett Sutton and the proud father of three daughters and 2 sons – Lemar, Janelle, Sasha, Malcolm, and Jenae

Quotes that Inspire Career Growth:

2 Corinthians 13:5 ESV

Examine yourselves, to see whether you are in the faith. Test yourselves. Or do you not realize this about yourselves, that Jesus Christ is in you?—unless indeed you fail to meet the test!

President Barack Obama

"Community colleges play an important role in helping people transition between careers by providing the retooling they need to take on a new career. "

Oprah Winfrey

"I'm sick of people sitting in chairs stating their problems. Then we roll the videotape... then we have our experts on the topic... I'm in the 'What's next?' phase of my career."

Michael Jordan

"I've missed more than 9000 shots in my career. I've lost almost 300 games. 26 times, I've been trusted to take the game winning shot and missed. I've failed over and over and over again in my life. And that is why I succeed."

Table of Contents

Look at Your Boss

Rehabilitation for Your Career

a. Sit down for five minutes… (a minute if you are on the clock) Look at your boss!
b. Is this a position you want to have?
c. Is this a position you do not want to have?

Once you answer those questions – after you take a hard look at what your boss does for a living. If this is not something you want to do – You need to make a change. If this is something you want to do, you need to make a change; either way it requires you take a look at your boss, take a look at yourself, and then make a change. You must do something. It requires **You** to take action.

The End

Really it's that simple!

Chapter 1 ➤

Rehabilitation of Your Career

What's the definition of rehabilitation?

Rehabilitation is about restoration. It is about making you fit again. When we look at the term rehabilitate, we typically relate it to physical injuries and habitual behavior. What we don't realize is that we can be injured within our career progression and opportunities in the same way that we can be injured by our physical injuries and habitual behavior. You can get injured due to no fault of your own or by your own negligence. I must point out that injuries due to your career progression and professional development are almost always self-inflicted injuries.

The word rehabilitate comes from the Latin word "rehabilitare" meaning to make fit again.

Webster's Dictionary Definition of Rehabilitation

"Rehabilitation is a treatment or treatments designed to facilitate the process of recovery from injury, illness, or disease to as normal a condition as possible."

Rehabilitation:

The freedictionary.com definition of Rehabilitate

re•ha•bil•i•tate
1. To restore to good health or useful life, as through therapy and education.
2. To restore to good condition, operation, or capacity.
3. To reinstate the good name of.
4. To restore the former rank, privileges, or rights of.

About a year ago (2011), I was at a church function at Tuckaseegee Park, in Mount Holly, N.C. – There was a skateboard park and at 48 years old I got on the skateboard – need I say more? - Broken leg, healing, rehabilitation. The injury was due to my negligence, the rehabilitation of the injury is what sticks with me. I put in countless hours to get myself back in shape – I was in a wheelchair for three months and I wanted to walk! It was not until a year later, when an incident occurred that I realized the magnitude of my rehabilitation. I dropped my car off at the shop to get my tires changed. I saw a Dunken' Donuts in the distance and attempted to cross a four lane highway to get something to eat! I was in the middle of the street, cars bearing down on me, and I went to run —and it was then that I realized I rehabbed to walk. I could not run! I scurried across the street... my heart pounding... I kept saying in my mind, I rehabbed to walk! When I sat down and ate my donut - The whole time I was thinking, Lord, how am I going to get back across the street? I rehabbed to walk! I completed my rehabilitation to walk!

When it comes to injuries in your career and professional development the injury can be due to what you

The whole time I was thinking, Lord, how I am I going to get back across the street.

have done or by what you have not done- It can also be attributed to what you have been motivated to do. My motivation was to walk – so I walked! We are not going to focus on the things that have prevented you from moving forward – You know those things far better than I do – The truth be told, You can probably fill up this book with more reasons for You not to succeed then I will put in this book for You to succeed.

You have had a number of reasons, concerns, and excuses that have prevented You from achieving the things You set out to achieve in your life; It could have been when you were in high school or college. Listen, I am not saying that You did not have legitimate reasons – However, my focus; our focus will be targeted at getting You to do something different. Our focus will be for You to take a hard look at yourself – For You to do a "check-up from the neck up!' For You to say I have had enough with my current situation! I want to make sure your career rehabilitation is not just putting you in a position to walk – I want you to run- I want you to move forward – I want You to not look back and position yourself to give back!

When we take a deeper look at the definition of rehabilitate we see that its primary function is to restore you back to good health – to let you operate in a useful capacity.

re•ha•bil•i•tate

1. To restore to good health or useful life, as through therapy and education.

When I speak to youth groups and individuals trying to get their lives back on track- I tell them to finish what they started. Sometimes that is as simple as going back to school to get a GED or as complicated as going back to college or taking a form of career training to reach their goal. I tell them not to go to college to get a hat and a t-shirt –

> *5 P's - Proper Planning Prevents Poor Performance*

Go to college to graduate! When I walk through the campus I always remind the students they are there to graduate – You have to go to college to complete your degree. A degree does not guarantee that you will succeed but it will prepare you and get you a step closer to success. Listen, now its time for you to finish what you started. If you never started college or career training – There is no better time to start then today. It is time for you to make a commitment to study and to become the expert at what you want to do, so you can make a move. Rehabilitation will require planning, sacrifice, and commitment. You plan your work and work your plan!

We had a saying in the military that went Proper Planning Prevents Poor Performance, the 5 P's. If you have been doing the "same ole, same ole' for so long that you believe that is enough, then it's time for you to look at your boss, look at yourself and begin the rehabilitation of your career.

Rehabilitation begins with the Consultation:

Okay – this will be the most difficult part, Self-Consultation! It is so easy for us to point out the faults in others. You can probably read your best friend or spouse up and down. But this consultation is about you reading 'You'. Don't pull any punches. First, I need you to take 'You' out of the picture and look at you. If you looked at your boss and you realize that you can be in a better position – You have to admit it. You have to say to yourself – "I can do better" – Then, You have to make a decision to do better! It starts with defining your strength and weaknesses. For whatever reason you have become a procrastinator. Oh you have good intentions but you just can't get started. Or you get started then you stop. If you did a proper check-up from the neck up then you identified yourself as a procrastinator – Oh I know you have your reasons...

The freedictionary.com definition of Consultation

con·sul·ta·tion☐
1. the act of consulting; conference.
2. a meeting for deliberation, discussion, or decision.
3. a meeting of physicians to evaluate a patient's case and treatment.

    The first step to rehabilitation is to admit that you have a problem. It is easy to point to the reasons that a problem exist, however, correction requires you to admit there is a problem. As a matter of fact, it requires you to say to 'You' that you are the problem.

    When you took those five minutes to look at your boss, what did you see? Did you see your boss as this all powerful figure from a futuristic movie? Or, did you see someone just like yourself that may have put in a little more time and a little more effort.

I work with some pretty amazing people and I found the most amazing thing about them is the time they invested in themselves. We will go to hell and back for a friend but throw ourselves to the waste side. Your consultation of yourself has to be purposeful and deliberate -

"A con•sul•ta•tion☐is a purposeful deliberate discussion that require you to make a decision."

Once you have looked at your boss – the next thing you have to do is look at You. It has to be deliberate! Yes, it requires you to make a decision. Do you want more? Stop! Do you? What has prevented you from taking the next steps in your life? If you are working a job that does not require a particular skillset and if your boss has that job unless you take a look at yourself – unless you make a change that job is in your future. You will move up to the job that your boss holds – the job that you despise. You will become that person. I am not saying your boss is not the nicest person in the world. I am simply asking you, do you want the job that your boss has? I am challenging you to make a change if you so desire. You have to admit you are in a situation you want to change. You have to make a declaration to change.

The Declaration - I have a problem!

The first step is to admit "I have a problem" – say that – look in the mirror and say "I have a problem, I do not like my current position and I am committed to making a change! I have looked at my boss and I do/do not want to be in that position. I know I have to make a change and my first step is..."

What is your problem??? What is your true concern??? Are you not happy with your job??? Are you not happy with your career??? Is your job not a career? Is your career feeling like a job??? Do you see all the question marks surrounding You??? You have to put yourself in the position to answer the questions – You have the answers – My goal is to get You to dig deep and get the answers.

The problem you are having with admitting you have a problem – the concern you are having with admitting you are not happy is you feed yourself what I call "happy nuggets"

Jamesism definition of a "Happy Nugget" A Happy Nugget is the self-imposed justifiable excuse for temporary happiness.

Example: It's when you hate your job and you say... "It's okay." – "It pays the bills." –

Or, When you say "I can't wait till Friday" on Sunday night.

Happy Nuggets are to the career deprived what "I will only take a sip" is to the alcoholic – It is faulty logic.

The problem with admitting there is a problem, especially with career rehabilitation, is we must move out of our comfort zone. We hear that term thrown around a lot – "Comfort Zone' - You may be locked in a place where you believe this is all you can ever achieve, this is all you will ever be, and this is who you are.

Take a minute to reflect on that last sentence... you are 20 years old and you just said "This is it!"- "That is all!" You could be 30 years old.... 40, 50, 60 years old... You feel you can't reinvent yourself – You feel you can't go through rehabilitation to restore yourself to a good condition. You may have taken a class... you got a degree... you restored yourself to the point of walking – but you need to run. You may believe this is it – 'You' may be saying to you "but this is who I am!" STOP!!! Look at your boss!!!

> *What did your boss do that you can't do?*

LOOK AT YOUR BOSS!

What did your boss do that you can't do? – The reality is You do the work - not your boss! Look at your boss and ask do I want to be in that position in the next 3 -5 years? Yes or No

If your response is 'yes' – what will it take for you to get there? What are the qualifications for the job? – If you respond 'no' – what does it take to get out of your current job – what job do you want? – If you are content with your current situation, put this book down; you're wasting your time. WAIT!!!

Wait!!! You might get inspired. No one can do this for you. No matter what your response, it requires you to take action. It requires you to make a change. If you are not content with your life; change. If you have lost your drive; get motivated.

When I was first injured before the ambulance arrived there were a bunch of people around me. There were people on the scene that had a medical background – I believe one was a nurse - The first thing she tried to do was apply the R.I.C.E Technique: Rest - Ice - Compression- Elevation. I heard her yelling to someone to get some ice. R.I.C.E Techniques are typically used when we are first injured and for minor injuries. Please understand your career injury is major - You have rested for the last however many years. I have to revise R.I.C.E for this occasion. You have to apply this refined redefined R.I.C.E. Technique now. You have to apply this new R.I.C.E Technique every day. As you try to pull yourself up and out of your current situation, you will find yourself with many minor injuries. You are going to pull back the wounds on a lot of things you have been dealing with for years. You will be emptying a bag of happy nuggets you have carried for a very long time.

They take their new found energy and work with it, not their excuses!

The New and Improved R.I.C.E:

R- Rejuvenate – Webster's definition of rejuvenate is to 'Restore to its Original State" - It is time for you to buy a case of 5-hour energy and get to work. I see hundreds of adult learners a week – They have jobs, they have responsibilities, they all have concerns and issues – But they have all been rejuvenated. They have made a pledge to change and they have taken steps to begin to change. It may hurt, but they were rejuvenated. They take their new found energy and work with it; not their excuses, their goals are to get things done! You have to re-establish yourself as someone that wants to improve. Your original state in high school or as far back as you can remember was to succeed. What stopped you? You can be rejuvenated; you just have to find something of interest you want to pursue.

> *My son Malcolm earned a Black Belt in Tae Kwon Do when he was 8 years old; he then got bored with it – He didn't want to go to the classes anymore and for the life of me I could not understand. He was a natural; He won state competitions with ease. I found out later that he was in it for the thrill of promotions. He was 14 when he picked up a guitar and in 4 months he played like he had it for years. He picked up the Bass and he was playing with the church youth band in 2 weeks. I then realized he needed to constantly be rejuvenated. He needed to be challenged or he was bored.*

What are you interested in doing? What became so mundane and boring to you that you stopped? What obstacle prevented you from moving forward?

The next step after being rejuvenated is to find the strength to pursue – You have to be invigorated.

I- Invigorating – You need to be invigorated – You have to impart that strength – You have to be full of energy – Once you past the place of being rejuvenated – You have to get to the place of being invigorating.

> *Jenae my dancer – My daughter Jenae is invigorating – She dances with a passion and a strength that draws you in. However, what is most impressive about my daughter is she had an issue with speech – She had to take speech therapy through the 6th grade – Yet; she excelled in all her classes. By the time she completed the 8th grade she competed in the National Beta Club speech competition and took fourth place. She rehabilitated to run – She found the strength to succeed.*

C- Confidence – Every time you take a step closer in your rehabilitation your confidence rises. Every time you make it to a personal check-point your confidence rises. One of the rehabilitation centers' I went to was called Phoenix Physical

Therapy. Their motto was they had "a passion to assist you with better living." They always talked about the "phoenix rising"- As

> *Every time you make it to a check-point your 'Phoenix Rises'.*

you build your confidence, your phoenix will rise. As your confidence grows get ready for your doubters to throw stones. I was a stone thrower. Yes, I was the person that filled someone's happy nugget bag – I didn't discourage anyone but I did find a way to have them question the decisions they made. But when I stopped throwing stones and started doing something to get myself together – Stones started flying my way. It is amazing how some people would call me cocky after I started completing my goals.

Jamesism: I say cockiness and confidence are like a walk on a high wire.

Yes, on days I will come across as cocky – but that simply means I surpassed my goal at my check point. I am feeling good! The Phoenix has risen! My confidence has soared! Stop!!! You should feel good right now - you didn't put this book down – This is the first time you made it this far with a motivational/self-help book. This is a check point for you. Be proud!

Confidence: When you are in the military you travel. What we don't hear about is the family that travels with you. My family never stayed in one location for more than 3 years. My wife held the family together by making our house our home. She supported me every time I told her I wanted to go back to school to get another degree. I went to school so much – After a while, she started asking me why I wasn't in school. My wife Jeannett was my first Life Coach – She held me accountable to my goals. She constantly boosted my confidence. Today she encourages everyone that comes her way – her confidence is the Prayer and confidence she instills in others.

> The only thing you really have control over in your life is your attitude...

E- Effervescent - The world dictionary defines effervescent as high-spirited; vivacious, a person that is happy – not just carrying around a bag of "happy nuggets" –But truly happy. Why did I pick the word effervescent? I wanted you to think. You see happiness just like unhappiness is controlled by what you think. The only thing you really have control over in your life is your attitude; how you adjust to the things around you. You may not be able to control the circumstance but you can control your reaction to the circumstance. Your Rehabilitation is your control of your situation – If you walk with your head up – You can't see the faults at your feet– If you can't see them you are less likely to act on them. You are less likely to let them dominate you.

My adult children Lemar, Janelle, and Sasha each live lives according to the things they have been taught. My hope is they remain high-spirited; that they apply the 'New R.I.C.E Principles' and have great success. I will continue to encourage them to extend their potential. They had some good life lessons and some life lessons that they must deal with today. If they ask my advice I will simply say to look at your boss, you at yourself, and do something! Are you on track to where you want to be?

Ok, You Ready?

It will take time. I speak to people every day that want that microwaveable success. I remember my nephew asking me how he can get my position. I told him to put God first… and then go to work on self-improvement. You have to put yourself on the clock- It is imperative that you create a timeline in which you want to achieve success. Implement the 5 P's -If you map it out you can see it, it becomes real. You have to plan your work, and work your plan.

Apply the R.I.C.E. techniques to your plan. When I was in college, I knew exactly when I needed to take a class and when to complete it. In the military, I knew when the next promotion board was and I knew the qualifications of the positions I wanted to hold. Are you ready? If you feel you're too young ... too old... turn to chapter 4 - It's never too late! Really go to Chapter 4!

Welcome back from Chapter 4. Did you enjoy the story? Good – now you know it can be done! You know that you can make a change. No matter how young or how old you are – You can make a change! You can make something positive happen in your life- you can go from being a store clerk to a technical analysis if you have a desire to change. Now go back to the Mirror - It is time to make a declaration for change – This is your declaration for 'You'. Not your family, not your friends – This is your declaration for 'You' – It's time to be specific.

> *The first step... "I have a problem" – say that – look in the mirror and say "I have a problem, I do not like my current position and I am committed to making a change! I have looked at my boss and I do/do not want to be in that position. I know I have to make a change and my first step is..."*

If you made that declaration then you can now go to the next chapter – If you did not make that declaration STOP!!! Don't move on! Do not pass "GO" -- If you are still not committed to making something happen or you feel you cannot make a change – If your bag of excuses.... I mean your bag of reasons or concerns are still preventing you from making a declaration to yourself – If your "happy nugget" bag is overflowing – go to chapter 5 – No Excuses!

Now what??? Jaime will be the first to tell you its hard – it takes sacrifice! It takes commitment! What are your excuses??? Ha! Are you ready to make that declaration? If you are, here we go:

The Declaration:

"I have a problem, I do not like my current position and I am committed to making a change! I have looked at my boss and I do/do not want to be in that position... I have read the 4th and 5th Chapter– I have been inspired to make that change- I know it will take commitment and leaving my comfort zone but I am ready! I know I have to make a change and my first step is..."

You can go to the next chapter... If you're still not ready, stop!!!

Still not convinced? Wow... your 'happy nugget' bag must really be overflowing. You are lukewarm! That means you are almost there – You just need to dive in! You are not sure that you can make it... You believe your own hype! You have talked to 'You' so much that you believe failure is an option – "Where is that coming from?" – Stop!!! You can put this book down but if you are on the bubble, turn to Chapter 6 'For the Saints' – We are about to go to church!

After reading Chapter 6 you understand that rehabilitating your career is a problem for a lot of people you are not alone. You just have to be one of the few willing to make the sacrifice to make improvements to yourself.

Change is Hard:

Change is hard... Change comes with obstacles – Change takes commitment -   Are you ready to make that commitment to you? Are you ready to make that declaration to yourself? Look in the mirror and say these words:

> *"I have a problem, I do not like my current position and I am committed to making a change! I have looked at my boss and I do/do not want to be in that position. I know I have to make a change and my first step is..."*

If you have made the declaration— you can turn to the next chapter.

Time to Move On!

If you have not made the declaration – Please understand I will not give up on you but 'You' have given up on yourself! Your family and friends have not given up on you.

> You have a defeatist attitude you have lost belief in yourself... Stop!!!

'You' have given up on yourself- You have a defeatist attitude, 'You' have lost the belief in you – Stop!!! Ask yourself what are the real reasons you are not trying to be more successful? What are you afraid of? Trying? Failing? You are not trying now so you're failing now! Duck!!! The nuggets are flying – I touched a nerve - I DID NOT CALL YOU A FAILURE!!! However, if you want something and you are not trying to get it; you are failing. It's time. You have to go to the next chapter – Yes, YES!!! Now you are ready for the second chapter. But not before we try to get you to say this declaration.

The Declaration:

"I do not like my current position and I am committed to making a change! I have looked at my boss and I do/do not want to be in that position. I know I have to make a change and my first step is to ...

Questions:

Did you look at your Boss? What did you see?

_____

_____

_____

_____

How many times did it take before you took the 'Declaration'? Why?

_____

_____

_____

_____

Do you think you are ready to Rehabilitation your Career? If so, explain why?

_____

_____

_____

List three of your most commonly used "Happy Nuggets" – What do you tell folk that you don't want to know you are unhappy with your job?

1._____

2._____

3._____

What are your impressions of the New and Improved R.I.C.E?

_____

_____

_____

What do you need to do to implement your New and Improved R.I.C.E?

_____

_____

_____

_____

Notes

_____

_____

_____

_____

_____

_____

_____

_____

_____

_____

_____

_____

_____

_____

_____

_____

_____

_____

Listen, everyone is not going to support you. You have to depend on you to make that change. Read the Scriptures!

Colossians 3:17 ESV

And whatever you do, in word or deed, do everything in the name of the Lord Jesus, giving thanks to God the Father through him.

Colossians 3:23 ESV

Whatever you do, work heartily, as for the Lord and not for men.

Proverbs 13:4 ESV

The soul of the sluggard craves and gets nothing, while the soul of the diligent is richly supplied.

Philippians 4:13 ESV

I can do all things through him who strengthens me.

Chapter 2 ⇒

What are your excuses for not being successful?

"What do you do-do?"
Bishop Waylyn Hobbs Jr.

Before you close this book and say "Ah Lawd, He going to Church on Us" Please understand that biblical principles are the foundation for success.

I understand that God is the foundation- I can do all things through Christ that strengthens me!

Jeremiah 29:11 *For I know the plans I have for you, declares the LORD, plans for welfare and not for evil, to give you a future and a hope.*

Psalm 18:32-34 *The God who equipped me with strength and made my way blameless. He made my feet like the feet of a deer and set me secure on the heights. He trains my hands for war, so that my arms can bend a bow of bronze.*

Ecclesiastes 9:10 [10] *Whatever your hand finds to do, do it with your might,[a] for there is no work or thought or knowledge or wisdom in Sheol, to which you are going.*

I want to encourage you to think when you look at the people that have impacted your life – don't just look at the person you asked to be your mentor – Actually, I have never asked anyone to be my mentor, I look at people that have impacted my life without knowing it. I look for people that have impacted my life based on what they have planted in me through their words and actions.

Let me introduce you to Bishop Waylyn Hobbs Jr., Senior Pastor at Coney Island Cathedral of Deliverance in Brooklyn N.Y., author of the book, "New Mind, New You!"

I remember a sermon that Bishop Hobbs preached and he said something that had a profound effect on my life. He said: "We don't do certain things anymore because we don't want to, but because we don't have the ability to do them anymore." Now this changed me because I had been in the military 17 years with three years to go before retirement. I had not completed my college degree and the military was paying 100% tuition. I had no excuse... but my happy nugget bag was full! hmmm - He said: "Stop telling people what you don't do and tell them what you do-do"

Now I know he was talking about throwing stones and not condemning people because we are not perfect. But what I received was "what do I do – do?" – What was I doing to impact my own life? I was one of those people that "hated on" or was concerned with what other people did but I was not applying myself to do better. Am I the only one that had that problem?

I had all the same excuses that I am hearing from you right now... Now I know I told you to keep your excuses to yourself but guess what? The excuses are the same! The excuses don't change! The same excuses I had, my children will have... The same excuses you have, your children will have. What excuses are you planting in your children? The excuses don't change. What is your excuse for not being successful? For not trying? What are you doing to make a change? Are you a chronic excuse maker? Do you feel the world is against you? If so, what are you doing about it? You say you can't do it? Why not?

I remember when I decided to finish college – I was sitting at the dinner table with my wife's family, I believe it was on Thanksgiving. I told them I was going to get my degree in Ministry. I knew that God had called me but I heard a few chuckles and I saw the expressions on their faces. Now I know they all loved and respected me but I wasn't the church going kind. I wasn't the 'holy roller" They responded based on my previous actions.

> *They responded based on my previous actions.*

I went to church but I didn't have the commitment and the zeal that is required for the kingdom. I went to warm a pew. Your actions dictate the reaction even from the people that love you.

I say that, to say this – Just because you decide to make a change does not mean that everyone will jump on board. Just because you decide to go back to school does not mean everyone will outwardly support you. For most of us, our friends and family have heard it all before. How many times have you said you were going to do something for yourself and didn't follow through? How many times did you start school or a business? You got a great idea... you started but never finished. How many promises have you broken to other people? How many promises have you broken to yourself? What??? The world is NOT going to stop because you decide it's time to get out of your stagnant position.

Bishop Hobbs doesn't even know the impact that he has had on my life. He doesn't know that a sermon meant to condemn those that were throwing stones actually converted a stone thrower. I realized my bag of nuggets was full. I was in the Air Force, I had a bunch of stuff going for me on the surface but in reality, I had completed very little. I was secure for the moment– I could do another 3 years and retire from the Air Force. But, after 3 years then what? I could collect my retirement check – I would be content but that was not going to be enough to sustain me – God had gifted me with more - I wanted more. I was tired of going through the motions! Are you tired? Are you tired of going through the motions – Is your bag of happy nuggets overflowing?

You have made a declaration to change, If you turned to this chapter without making the declaration, go to Chapter 7 – read my story – Bishop Hobbs always said "I am not there yet, but I am closer then I was." Please understand I am not there... that is why I always work to get better – and as I get older, I shift to make people around me better. I love the fact that I am closer then I was! I found the more I achieved, the higher I raised the bar! Raise your bar. No one is going to raise your bar for you. Look at your boss! If you are ready to make that declaration - look in the mirror and say with conviction...

"I have a problem, I do not like my current position and I am committed to making a change! I have looked at my boss and I do/do not want to be like that. I know I have to make a change and my first step is to "Determine my Range of Motion"

Range of Motion:

After I broke my leg I had to go through Physical Therapy. Every time the Physical Therapist showed up at my house, we began with stretches. Then, after those painful warm-up stretches – she would give me a minute to rest and then she would check my range of motion. She would allow me to bend my leg and then she would push down a little harder to extend my reach pass my comfort zone. We touched on the level of our comfort zone earlier in the book. Your comfort zone is your current state, it's where you are right now; whether you consider yourself successful or not. Your comfort zone is not your measure of success – Your comfort zone is a place you won't surpass because of fear or anxiety – the unknown makes a lot of people nervous. I've found the best way for me to get pass my comfort zone was to be prepared. Something about them 5 P's! I had to know the direction of the progress. It was easier for me to push past the pain when I knew the objective and the outcome we were trying to achieve.

You have completed your declaration- Did you mean it? Now you have to create steps for

> *You have to figure out what you are capable of doing right now.*

change. Rehabilitation of your career goals will require you to figure out your comfort zone. Then, you have to push a little harder to extend pass your comfort zone. You can only move out of your current situation if you know what situation is. You have to figure out what are you capable of doing right now. Where is your motion? What is your current range of motion? You can push pass your comfort zone! Career rehabilitation is a process – the process is simple but it requires us to make a change. I've read a bunch of books that complicate a simple process.

Follow these Steps:

Step 1 –

Does your plan require college degree or training? Listen - It does require research!

You looked at your boss, you know what you want to do but you are unsure of the credentials required. If you have a good relationship with your boss; ask your boss! I have found that people love to talk about and share their accomplishments with someone that has an interest. If the relationship does not allow for this conversation, go online, go to the library, or go to the company website. You have to pull up job titles and job descriptions for the field you want to grow in. Please understand this is not an overnight process. You are just at the initial step of your rehabilitation. You are simply assessing the problem and looking for solutions. Research will be one of your greatest assets because if you start out by wasting time you will add more junk to your 'Happy Nugget' Bag. Procrastinators are easily discouraged.

Step 2 –

What do you have to cut out to make time?

Once you have determined the requirements for your career direction, you have to map out a plan for success. Utilizing the 5 ps will simplify your plan. Remember to plan your work and work your plan. You have to take a hard look at your schedule and move some things around. You have to make time for you. Guess what, someone will be upset- Someone will feel neglected – Keep your support system close and informed about your decision for change. You will get more support based on your actions then you will from your conversation. They heard it before! Why are you mad at them? You already looked at your boss; now look at 'You' – Yea, the Big 'Y. O. U."!

Step 3 –

What is my timeline for completion?

You must! You must! You must! You must Set Goals and Check Points; Create specific timelines. You need to plan your success. "Plan your work and work your plan" – I have been around some great people, they had some great ideas. They had written plans, all the details worked out – They had plans for their plan – What they didn't have was a commitment to work their plan. They didn't follow their plan. Set goals with specific check points. You need to have a built in timeline for your progress checks. When I started working on my Bachelor's degree, I knew when every class had to be taken and when I had to take them. I harassed my education counselor – I was always the first to know of any schedule changes. You are the adjuster of your life.

Side Bar - You must evaluate your progress – You must establish specific goals with specific progress checks. – You must give yourself credit for any forward movement. Here are some progress checks examples:

1. I Looked at my Boss! (I did not roll my eyes!)
2. I Researched Job Descriptions!
3. I Enrolled in School!
4. I **completed** my first class!
5. I told my friend "No", I had to study!

Jamesism: We celebrate completion! You have to line up the 'I's' and the 'ed's' – I completed!

You get the picture? – If the word 'I' is not at the beginning of the statement of completion and if the letters 'ed' is not at the end of the statement, there is no cause for celebration. Yes, you can clap when you are trying – You can clap in the midst of doing something to get excited; but the applause comes at the end of the show, the applause comes at completion. 'You' must line up the 'I's' and the 'ed's'- and say, "**I** complet**ed...**" - Every step you take forward, the 'Happy Nugget' Bag gets lighter.

Remember, you may miss a few family functions along the way. But in the end, you can have a big party to celebrate your accomplishments. You will hear the applause.

Whoa... I hear you – this process can feel a little overwhelming – because change will be a little uncomfortable! You cannot use the effects of change to fill your Happy Nugget Bag – You knew this was going to be uncomfortable - I told you it would! Whoa... If this is too much take a breath there are other

> *You knew this was going to be uncomfortable - I told you it would!*

options to help you get started. This is not the time to say no way! Stop!!! If this process is overwhelming find a life coach.

Life Coach

Your life coach is a specialist – not the general practitioner – your life coach is your career personal trainer. Life coaches write you a prescription and help you assess your "range of motion" – They will provide you with a one on one consultation in regard to your needs and specific goals. I have attended seminars and I have invited speakers to come to present to our student population.

I spent time with Craig Thompson former NFL player, CEO of Big Tyme Speaking and Coaching and Demetra Moore, Life Coach and Founder of "Moore Out Of Life" in Charlotte, NC – and hearing them both speak; I found that a life coach can assist you in making those critical decisions to change... I attended a seminar sponsored by Miss Moore and I found that many of the participants were individuals recreating their lives. They were individuals that were in rehabilitation of their careers. She explained to the group how she walked her clients through the process and provided feedback based on the individual's needs and direction. She becomes your personal trainer for the rehabilitation of your career!

Life coaches will provide individual assessments and career direction for those unsure of the direction they want to go. They go beyond peeling back the onion. They are detailed and specific. Be honest! If you are not self-sufficient - if you need someone else to hold you accountable; you may want to consider reaching out to a life coach. As I stated before my wife Jeannett was life coach. She held me accountable and kept me focused. Most life coaches will offer some form of a free seminar to introduce their services. Now you take that excuse out of your "happy nugget bag."

Next, you may have someone that you have a great relationship with; that you look up to, someone that can sit down and help you empty that happy nugget bag.

Mentors

Mentors are individuals that have expertise they want to share!

If you have a good relationship with someone you aspire to be like professionally or you know someone that works in the profession you would like to be in, you can approach them and ask them to become your mentor. Mentors are individuals that have expertise and they want to share the expertise with someone else. From my experience, mentors would like to see that you have already made some form of commitment to change and/or progress.

Also, understand the key phase in mentor – they must want to and have the desire to share information with someone else. You will add more nuggets to your bag if you ask someone to be your mentor that does not have a desire to be a mentor.

Typically, you can gauge if someone wants to be a mentor based on their actions. They would have already planted seeds in your life – They would have recognized your happy nugget bag is full... and they would already have their hands in your bag trying to remove them.

You may have a mentor in your life that you have no contact with but based on their actions and their story, you try to emulate them. Some would say that Oprah was their mentor yet she is someone they have never met but can aspire to be.

When I was 16, I worked in the mailroom for an advertising agency; my boss was 46 years old. During one of our conversations, we discussed the qualifications for his job. He had not completed high school and at the time I was not doing very well in school. I was getting straight D's just passing and failing some classes. I realized from that conversation that if I wanted to make something of my life, I would have to complete my education and take everything to the next level. Now don't get me wrong, I appreciate the fact that he took the time to have those conversations with me. He was one of my greatest mentors. I can also tell from those conversations, that he wanted me to make something more out of my life. It is from those conversations and from numerous other life experiences, that I have received the thought process for this book. If you are a person that is not content with where you are in your life- look at your boss; then turn to YOU!

Mentors are great!

Jamesism: The only problem I have with mentors that are appointed is they may just put on their happy face when you are around.

But for the Life Coach, it is their passion, their livelihood. The mentors in your life should live a life you want to aspire to be from what you have seen from "your line of sight." They may not even know you are watching. By the way, who is watching you?

The Declaration:

"I do not like my current position and I am committed to making a change! I have looked at my boss and I do/do not want to be in that position. I know I have to make a change and my first step is to "Determine my Range of Motion" – my second step is to "Build up my Strength" – The final step is to Put it All Together!"

Questions:

What is your 'Range of Motion'? How far do you push?

_____

_____

_____

_____

What are your goals?

_____

_____

_____

_____

Do you think you will benefit from a life coach? Explain why?

_____

_____

_____

List three of your most commonly used "Happy Nuggets" – What is keeping you

1._____

2._____

3._____

Who are the mentors you have in mind? How many from a distance? Name them!

_____

_____

_____

Notes

_____

_____

_____

_____

_____

_____

_____

_____

_____

Listen – With everything you have read or heard it all comes down to you making a change. You will have the greatest impact on you. Read the Scriptures!

2 Thessalonians 3:10-12 ESV

For even when we were with you, we would give you this command: If anyone is not willing to work, let him not eat. For we hear that some among you walk in idleness, not busy at work, but busybodies. Now such persons we command and encourage in the Lord Jesus Christ to do their work quietly and to earn their own living.

Colossians 3:1-25 ESV

If then you have been raised with Christ, seek the things that are above, where Christ is, seated at the right hand of God. Set your minds on things that are above, not on things that are on earth. For you have died, and your life is hidden with Christ in God. When Christ who is your life appears, then you also will appear with him in glory. Put to death therefore what is earthly in you: sexual immorality, impurity, passion, evil desire, and covetousness, which is idolatry. ...

Chapter 3 ➤

Good Pressure

"No Pain, No Gain"

Anyone that has been through rehabilitation for any reason will tell you it hurts! The worst part about rehabilitation is beginning - the initial pain is excruciating - Awww – I cringe just thinking about it. Rehabilitation begins before the injury is healed. As a matter of fact, rehabilitation begins at the end of the surgery. The doctor verifies your range of motion – they check your bodily functions before you are released from the hospital.

I started rehabilitation for my injured leg less than a week after the injury. When the Physical Therapist called and said she was coming over, I said "For What? "When she showed up at my door, I pretended I was sleep; I pretended it hurt to the point of exhaustion. It was extremely painful for me to move my leg. I didn't know what she planned to do but I wanted no part of it.

Stop!!!

Your Career Rehabilitation will not be without pain and sacrifice. It will be uncomfortable – It will hurt. It will be painful for you to begin rehabilitation of your career. We just peeled back the onion a little.

You have a bag full of "happy nuggets." You might be at a place where you allowed the healing to begin before the rehabilitation. Or you may be at a place where you just sat there and the healing is finished but the rehabilitation never took place. The nurse kept telling me if you don't do it now, you will pay for it later– If you don't flex now... If you don't try to walk now... If you don't put pressure on it now... it is going to hurt more. Career Rehabilitation is going to hurt – It is going to hurt more because you did not apply pressure to your career goals for years!

We are all familiar with the term "No Pain, No Gain." The hard thing about beginning a workout routine is the pain the next day... the Pain! You may be sore for a few days or a week, maybe more. When you begin your career rehabilitation routine it will take some time for you to adjust. Your body and your mind will feel a pressure you have not experienced since grade

> *They take their new found energy and work with it, not their excuses!*

school. Give yourself time to adjust; your body will get use to the pressure you are putting it through. It is going to hurt!

Good Pressure – is painful at first – huh? The first time I put my leg off the bed and tried to stand up, I experienced the most excruciating pain I have ever experienced in my life. The blood rushed down my leg and I let out a scream. I immediately jumped (well crawled) back on the bed and elevated my leg. I spoke to a woman that experienced the same thing. She had the same injury and she said when she put her foot down and felt the pain, it was like she was going to give birth through her foot.

The first time you attempt to make a change in your career status, you will want to jump back on the bed with your bag of happy nuggets clutched to your chest. The experience of career rehabilitation is painful. You are trying to release yourself from something you carried for a long time.

At this point you may be saying ouch-Believe it when I say that's good! We know you are alive. I yelled, I screamed, I even got mad at my physical therapist. I think I owe her an apology. You know what she did? She calmly said "ok, Mr. Sutton (pause) Ok, let's go ahead and stand up now!"

Stand up – You have made a declaration! You have looked at your boss! You are ready for a change! You know your 'range of motion' - I found after a few weeks my 'range of motion' increased – it was time to build strength. Psst... It is never too late to start your rehabilitation for your career.

Listen, I can draw this chapter out longer but I want you to read the book –I want you to finish this book but most importantly, I want you to take action.

No Pain, No Gain – It's going to hurt! It is going to be painful – I know I said it a hundred times –

What am I telling you that you don't already know. What I am telling you is what you won't accept –

It's You!

Before this book came to the presses, I had a few people review it to see if the content was relevant – Lady Reign, author of "Destined to Be" and "Deception of Life" gave me some insight to what I needed to do – She is a published author – I was excited to hear her call my notes a book.

Here is the conversation (no edits):

> *Lady Reign: the declaration is elaborated well, however, I don't get it when you say look at your boss, the boss is not the problem, the person and their unhappiness is the problem. We can't look at someone else and try to figure out what's wrong with ourselves, we have to look deep within so I think on the declaration instead of saying look at your boss it should say look in the mirror or look within. Ok say we are looking at the boss, what are we looking at and why? What if our perception is this man is happy and got it all together, but how do we know that. He could go home and sit in the corner and cry. The problem with looking at other people is it's all about perception. (see the movie Good Deeds)*

James: Thank You, I'm still exited because you referred to my notes as a book- I will make some changes and try to get the' look at your boss' 'concept clarified- I agree we need to ultimately look at ourselves but I want folk to identify with the person that they see at work every day- to look at the person they work for and work with to decide if they want to be the supervisor - Or do they want to take another career path. I clearly didn't get that point across.

You see the pain is identifying you are the problem; the boss is just a <u>professional measuring stick</u> – If you look at your boss and you say "I can do his job" and then you look at his job description and it requires a certain credential – You may want the job, You may be able to do the job but the reality is you are qualified for the job.

> *The boss is just a professional measuring stick –*

The pain will be associated with you going back to get that qualification whether it is specific training or a college degree. I remember during a feedback session with one of my students – he told me he looked at his boss and said he could do the job but he didn't have the certification – I asked him why he didn't have the certification – His response was he didn't want to go back to school – I told him he didn't want the job! After speaking with him further, I realized that he really wanted a job like his boss. He just didn't want to deal with the pain of returning to school. He wanted the position but he didn't want to do the work. It would be too painful to adjust his hours etc. Now I believe 'Favor ain't fair' – but 'Faith without works is dead'. We all heard the phrase "You see the Glory, but don't know the Story" – most successful people have worked hard to get what they want!

I ran into a member at my church today Chris, He had been out of work for over a year. When he found a job he told me that what impressed the hiring manager the most is that he had completed some schooling. He didn't just sit at home filling his 'happy nugget bag'. He was 'Do –Doing It' Wait, I forgot to tell you, the reason he approached me was he was hiring three people. He rehabbed to run!

We are headed to Chapter 4 – It's Never Too Late! Some of you have read that chapter already – You followed directions! If you already read it – Read it again! - Because reading this book has put a few new happy nuggets in your bag. They are called 'doubt' and 'uncertainty' – 'Patience!'

Jamesism: 'Don't be patient, patient people wait, impatient people do!'

Understand it is never too late to begin the Career Rehabilitation process – We do it for different reasons. Sometimes it is simply I am bored and unfulfilled. It's never too late!

The Declaration:

"I do not like my current position and I am committed to making a change! I have looked at my boss and I do/do not want to be in that position. I know I have to make a change and my first step is to "Determine my Range of Motion" – my second step is to "Build up my Strength" – The final step is to Put it All Together!"

Questions:

What is your pain? Are you ready for the hurt?

_____

_____

_____

_____

Can you make a stand? What is stopping you?

_____

_____

_____

_____

What wound do you have to overcome to move forward? What habit do you have to break or mend?

_____

_____

_____

_____

List three of your most commonly used "Happy Nuggets" – These prevent you from starting.

1._____

2._____

3._____

Notes

_____

_____

_____

_____

_____

_____

_____

_____

_____

_____

Chapter 4 ➤

It's Never Too Late!

"It's never too late!"

When I began my rehabilitation on my leg – I started rehab immediately following the injury. Once I started to increase my range of motion – we moved to strength exercises – The Physical Therapist would leave me with a bunch of

> *It is never too late to begin the Career Rehabilitation Process –*

instructions and exercises to do during the week and I would do them a hour before she came... She would ask if I did my exercises and I would say 'yea" – But I was hurting myself – The strength building is the most important part of rehabilitation – This is where you are if you made it this far. That is the reason I couldn't run! I didn't have the strength. I went through the motions.

Stop going through the motions. I see student's every day that enrolls in college then dropout. They create more debt and they dig a deeper hole. There are no short-cuts – There are no handouts – there is work and dedication. Talent is not a shortcut, its talent.

You've done the research... You have a plan or a desire to do something – You understand the skill set that is required to make a move –Now if you have been so engrossed in this book that you have not done any research – This book is now a "happy nugget" – give me a few more moments then this book will be removed from your happy nugget bag and placed on your shelf.

I want to tell you about a man I came in contact with not so long ago. He began his rehabilitation 25 years after his initial blow. He completed HS had a family and worked as a stock clerk for 33 years. When his kids started moving out – he decided he wanted something different. He put enough cans on the shelf for a lifetime and his boss's got younger and younger. He wanted to sit down and enjoy his day like everyone else. He shared with me that he wasn't sure he could do it because of his age (60) - but every day he attended a class his confidence and his will to succeed increased.

Did I mention he was 60 years old? What made him special was not just the fact that he was 60 years old. What made him special is that he acted on his will to change. He decided on the technology degree and he could barely use a computer. Now, he has the ability to fix them. His career rehabilitation began and he applied the New R.I.C.E. techniques. If you ever put ice on an injury, you will find it is uncomfortable. You move the bag around so much the ice melts. But he kept that ice pack on his injury and saw the results of his 'happy nugget bag' get empty.

There are hundreds of stories of individuals that have been back to school – The over comers, the achievers, the conquerors. They are just like you – They could be you. But You have to make the change.

Rehabilitation II:

When I realized I could not run I knew I had to begin the rehabilitation process again. I brought my gym bag to work and it stayed under my desk for a week. The first time I got on the stationary bike – I rode it for 5 minutes. It was okay! After I went back to my desk and sat down for about ten minutes it hurt. My muscles started to cramp up. I started getting spasms. It hurt! It was pretty bad! Now it wasn't like the initial physical therapy it had a whole new set of problems. It hurt! The next day, I had to start a new Tylenol and Advil regiment.

Starting over after an injury heals is painful. In some cases the doctor may have to re-break the original break to let the healing process start from the beginning. Fortunately for you, your rehabilitation only requires you to strengthen the skills you already have. In some cases, it will require your range of motion to extend past what you are accustomed to doing. The only breaking that needs to be done is old habits.

The fact that you have read the book to this point is good. I give you a credit for that. Put a feather in your hat! I am going to say it –whew! – I just let out a breath. The reality is until you make a move and until you do some research to make a change, until you take the declaration and commit to yourself. You are just like this book; words! Your actions are nothing but words. Tough Love!

Remember, I carried my gym bag for a week before I started my new rehabilitation to run. You may carry this book around for a week, a month, a year (if so pick up the new edition). My hope is that this book finds a shelf and you use your notes. That you use your new found energy to make something happen. It's time to run.

It is really simple if you keep the declaration:

"I do not like my current position and I am committed to making a change! I have looked at my boss and I do/do not want to be in that position. I know I have to make a change and my first step is to "Determine my Range of Motion" – my second step is to "Build up my Strength" – The final step...

Questions:

Do you feel it's too late for you to make a change?
How old is too old?

_____

_____

_____

_____

Look at your recent failures? Why did you fail?

_____

_____

_____

_____

Do you think you are ready to Rehabilitation your
Career? If so, explain why?

_____

_____

_____

List three of your most commonly used "Happy Nuggets" – What do you have to do to begin all over again?

1._____

2._____

3._____

Notes

_____

_____

_____

_____

_____

_____

_____

_____

_____

_____

_____

_____

_____

_____

Look at Your boss!   page 63

Chapter 5 ➤

No Excuses!

Jaime

Once you embark on the journey of 'Rehabilitating your Career' – It is important to have balance or you put more nuggets in your bag then you remove. When I really started getting into my physical therapy – I started building strength in my legs – the physical therapist had me using weights and I felt myself getting better – it was still painful – When I starting doing the exercises the pain was intense but it gradually subsided as I performed the motions. It still hurt; Yes, I still pretended it hurt a little more than it did; so she would take it easy. But the physical therapist has been there before –she wasn't buying it. I wasn't her first broke leg. It was my first broke leg, but she saw it all before; I couldn't give her a bunch of lip service. That is where a life coach or mentor comes in to play; they have heard it all before.

Jaime - Jaime is a single Mom, she has two beautiful daughters, she has a full time job, she works an internship, and she has just completed her Master's Degree in-residence. She is also active in her church – she teaches children's church – and her girls are her shadow. She finds time to spend quality time with her daughters. I want to point out that Jaime only has 24 hours in her day. For the last year, I have seen Jaime in action – I am talking about the New R.I.C.E. Techniques in all its glory; Rejuvenated, Invigorating, Confidence, and Effervescent. I hear your murmurings. "Well, she ain't special she is no different than anyone else" – Exactly! So James, "What makes her story spectacular?" Simple! She is doing it! And 'You' are just reading this book talking about it – You are throwing stones at her and she is emptying her bag. Jaime will be the first to tell you with all she is juggling and with all she is doing, she ain't got time for "happy nuggets"- she can't fit them on her plate. She is 'do-doing' it! The question you should be asking yourself is what is so spectacular about you? Why are you 'Not' do-doing it?

> *"Well, she ain't special she is no different than anyone else – Exactly!"*

Balance and Proprioception – When I was going through my rehabilitation, what struck me as odd is I broke the right leg and the physical therapist had me working out the left leg too – She said I needed balance – Then she threw some funny big word at me – Proprioception – What?!? I still can't pronounce it - I asked her what the word Proprioception meant. Of course I was glaring at her! Okay! I threw a stone! She said that Proprioception was the minds way of consciously and unconsciously adjusting to the balance of the body – "Yea right" – it hurt; on both sides!

Finding your balance and proprioception is going to be an important element for you to succeed. You are going to have to juggle. You will miss some special events... You will miss the big game. You will lose a lot of sleep. And with the gas prices you will miss a little money too. But in the end it is the balance that will set you up for success. You are teaching yourself a valuable life lesson. If you can manage your time, you can manage that corporation's time. You can manage your business; you can manage your employees. When your strength is balanced you create options. A degree does not guarantee success. Proper Planning Prevents Poor Performance. Plan for your success. Plan for your future. Now didn't that sound good when I said your business and your employees? Ask Chris - It starts with work – It starts with getting rid of the thoughts that say you can't – Listen - No excuses!

The Declaration:

"I do not like my current position and I am committed to making a change! I have looked at my boss and I do/do not want to be in that position. I know I have to make a change and my first step is to "Determine my Range of Motion" – my second step is to "Build up my Strength" – The final step is to ...!"

Questions:

Do you think there are any legitimate excuses for not making a change if you are not happy?

_____

_____

_____

_____

Is there a difference between an excuse and a reason?

_____

_____

_____

_____

What do you have to balance to make a change work?

_____

_____

_____

List three of your most commonly used "Happy Nuggets" – Who do you feel you will let down if you embark on change?

1._____

2._____

3._____

Notes

_____

_____

_____

_____

_____

_____

_____

_____

_____

_____

Listen, you can do it – you have to be your primary support. Stop trying to depend on people – Let go and Let God! Read the Scriptures!

Philippians 4:13 ESV

I can do all things through him who strengthens me.

Colossians 3:24 ESV

Knowing that from the Lord you will receive the inheritance as your reward. You are serving the Lord Christ.

Philippians 2:14-15 ESV

Do all things without grumbling or questioning, that you may be blameless and innocent, children of God without blemish in the midst of a crooked and twisted generation, among whom you shine as lights in the world,

Chapter 6 ➡️

For the Saints

"Who told you that?"

> *Proverbs 1:5 (AMP) The wise also will hear and increase in learning, and the person of understanding will acquire skill and attain to sound counsel [so that he may be able to steer his course righty]*

We will also increase in learning, acquire skill, and have a direction. There is something powerful about the word 'also'. It requires us to do more. Don't get me wrong, God's Word is enough – But it also requires us to do more. Did you hear all those stones hit the floor? – I offended "Duh Saints"

> *"Duh Saints" –Jamesism definition of the 'duh saints' - The folk that have bags and bags of happy nuggets laced with scripture – By lacing it with scripture it gives them even more perceived validation for their happy nuggets. 'Duh'*

I won't go to church on you but I know that there are a lot of spiritual people suffering from the same situation in regard to rehabilitating of their careers. Shhhhh– Let's stay focused. Now I ain't judging or throwing stones, I am beyond that place in my life; Almost. I am simply stating a fact. There are a lot of people struggling – from my perception – My perception is my reality! - I don't want to offend anyone so I will jump right in.

Pastor Tim McCarn is the Senior Pastor of Core Church, Mount Holly, N.C. And one of the things that have always amazed me about Pastor Tim is his ability to ask folk 'why"- Why do you have a defeatist mindset. He would ask—"who told you that?" – "Where did you get that from?"

During my final weeks of rehabilitation – The physical therapist specialist was pushing me harder. She had me walking downstairs and upstairs – She walked me down the hall throughout my house. Then she said – It's time to go outside and walk up the hill – I thought she was crazy! I know I looked at her like she was crazy, But she simply said Mr. Sutton you have to get over that hill. I cannot sign you off until you can walk up the hill. I wanted to be signed off. I wanted to be finished. Many thoughts ran through my mind – Do I fake the pain or do I work through the pain.

When you begin your career rehabilitation you are going to want to fake an injury – pretend there is more pain then you actually feel. Your 'excuse creativity' will flourish. You will be able to convince yourself a hundred ways of why you cannot make it to class – why you cannot complete a task. 'You' will tell you that you really don't need that certificate.

'You' will ask you "Is that $5,000 dollar raise worth the hassles?" You will get to the point where 'You' will surface and convince you that you are not

> *It's time for you to take the hill!*

worthy of your success. Who told you that? You!!!

The Physical Therapist just stood there not saying a word. She had her hand on the door and the other hand on her hip. After contemplating all the excuses – I started thinking about the reasons I needed to complete this task. I wanted to walk. But it all came down to this final thought. I wanted her to sign me off so I never had to see her again! – So, I took the hill!

It's time for you to take the hill! You cannot be afraid to take the next step in your rehabilitation – you have to rehab to run. When you reach out and get plugged into your desired program, your desired career choice, the day you walk in the door of your first class or the day you take that certification test and pass; Listen, the day you are lining up with other people in the rehabilitation process is the day you can get signed off.

Now you are at the check point where you are not looking at your boss as much. You are looking at yourself and your own accomplishments. Your "happy nugget" bag is getting lighter. It's getting harder for you to find a stone because your plate is full. When I got around like minded people, people looking to make a positive change in their life, my classmates, family, and friends, I was even more motivated to succeed. I wasn't alone and I could see that I wasn't alone.

When I broke my leg, I had a 'broke leg buddy '– Marcus. Ironically, my friend Marcus had crushed his ankle a week before I broke my leg – If you need any confirmation to my plight in rehabilitation he will confirm it – We spent many nights and early mornings 'praying, texting, texting scripture, talking, complaining about our wives, and crying to each other. We were encouraging and relating to each other because although other people saw us going through this situation and although they may have experienced a broken leg some time ago in their life, Marcus was going thought it with me now, he was actually living and experiencing my pain first hand. He was living it at the same pace as me. It was relevant. When you begin your rehabilitation, your classmates and instructors will work with you. They will feed off of your motivation and you will feed off of theirs.

I had an opportunity to meet other individuals going through healing via the internet and during my hospital appointments. The only thing we did when we saw each other was encourage each other – who told you that you were not a conqueror – Who told you that you can't be successful – Who told you that you shouldn't get an education – Who told you that? Who told you to stop trying to improve yourself? Who told you that your career rehabilitation was going to be easy? Who told you that you couldn't do it?

Proverbs 1:5 (AMP) The wise also will hear and increase in learning, and the person of understanding will acquire skill and attain to sound counsel [so that he may be able to steer his course righty]

The wise will understand they need to acquire the skill. This is going to hurt —According to Webster's Dictionary, Acquire means 'to come to have as a new or added characteristic, trait, or ability sustained by effort' – Ouch! If you put forth the effort it will be paid back with results.

The Declaration:

"I do not like my current position and I am committed to making a change! I have looked at my boss and I do/do not want to be in that position. I know I have to make a change and my first step is to "Determine my Range of Motion" – my second step is to "Build up my Strength" – The final step is...!"

Questions:

Do you believe it is ok for the 'Duh Saints' to do nothing to progress their career? Now we know 'He is Able" –But what is our responsibility?

_____

_____

_____

_____

Who told you that you can't succeed?

_____

_____

_____

_____

Where did you receive the mentality it is ok to be unhappy with your job?

_____

_____

_____

_____

_____

List three of your most commonly used "Happy Nuggets" – What scriptures do you use to justify where you are in life? Based on your self-admitted unhappiness?

1._____

2._____

3._____

Notes

_____

_____

_____

_____

_____

_____

_____

_____

_____

_____

_____

Look at Your boss!

Chapter 7 ➤

My Story

"Pride, Dignity, and Respect"
James Sutton Sr., My Dad

My father would wake me, my brother and sisters up at 2 or 3 in the morning when he came in from work and talk to us about "pride, dignity, and respect." I am not sure if it was because it was three o' clock in the morning or because he did it so often; but it stuck. Thanks to my father, I always carry myself with pride, dignity, and respect.

Yes, even folk with a good foundation require career rehabilitation. When I broke my leg I prepared myself to walk, I rehabilitated myself to walk. I always have to say that twice – flashbacks of that car bearing down on me (smh). Your story may be you did not complete your rehabilitation or your rehabilitation never started. You may be mentally positioned to walk but you want to run.

My Story – I received my bachelor's degree when I was 42 years old, one year before I retired from the military. I saw enough! I wanted to prep myself.

It was Hard! – It was tough... My 'happy nugget' bag was latched to my back pocket – I put on the happy face and reached back a few times to pull out a nugget every now and again. When I talked to someone I had my 'happy nugget' bag close by. Then the most amazing thing happened – I received my first grade –'A' – yes, you read that right – I got an 'A' – the first 'A' I could remember receiving since elementary school. Can you say 'COCKY?' – I mean confident! The phoenix was rising' – I felt good – The New R.I.C.E was in full effect. I graduated with my Bachelor's Degree Magna Cum Laude 3.88 GPA – this from the straight 'D' student in high school - Wow!

Don't Stop! – Now as you can see from my Bio I have five degrees and I am working toward my Doctorate in Organization Leadership – My rehabilitation of my career turned into my lifestyle – I gained a thirst for knowledge- I already had what my father instilled in me. I realized my problem was me – I have a saying "It ain't bragging, if you done it" – I done it, and I am still do-doing it. I am not there yet but I am closer then I was. My advice to you 'Don't Stop – Do-Do it'! - I was 45 years old when I received my first Master's Degree 3.9 GPA and 50 when I received my second Master's Degree!

Side Bar -Military Service:

Most of the people I have met during my 23 years in the United States Air Force had to rehabilitate their careers. Sometimes, the military job does not equate to its civilian counterpart without additional certifications or even a college degree. When someone retires from the military, they have typically reached the management level – their civilian counterpart has reached that level as well, however, the civilians tend to have additional credentials and/or have tenure with the company. That is why I tell all the former veterans I come into contact with, they need to complete their college degree or get their certifications. They need to know the requirements before they get out of the military.

Sorry, I know I got side tracked but a lot of military folk don't really know what to expect when they reach the civilian sector.

> *I got side tracked but a lot of military folk don't really know*

   One of the primary reasons I went back to school to finish my degree was when I ran into a retired Chief Master Sgt – he had reached the top of the enlisted military ranks –and he was packing bags at the commissary (grocery store) Yea – I threw stones. I asked him why he wasn't doing something else and he told me candidly that he didn't prepare. He told me that he didn't really want to work hard when he retired. Packing bags??? Not stones, truth! I was still dealing with that stuff. Then the "what do you do-do?" sermon resurfaced in my mind. I asked myself a question. Did I want to be a grocery bagger when I retired after 23 years of service? I looked at my boss! I knew I wanted to run!

My Acknowledgment Page

I have had some amazing 'not-mentors' in my life- Individuals that have impacted my decision to continue my education. I had some help to pursue my personal goals. You have help! You have a bunch of people that have been telling you for years, that you need to do something. But 'You' keep telling you they need to 'mind their own business!'

Why am I going to talk about these people? What do they have to do with this book? What do they have to do with looking at your boss?

They are important because they have been important. They were the people that reached into my 'happy nugget' bag and pulled out a handful of nuggets every time I came in contact with them. There are too many to name because I had a huge 'happy nugget' bag but it didn't prevent me from achieving my goals.

My Inspirations:

I have two brother-in-laws that have inspired me in my transition from the military to civilian life – Now all of my family has been helpful (this is my family disclaimer) but I have to talk about – Tony and Sean! I would have conversations about my transition from the military with them and they both encouraged me to continue my education – They confirmed to me that I had a worthy skill set and they both let me know that education validated what I already knew – Now I 'happy nuggeted' them to death. When I would call they didn't throw stones – They took a hand full of 'happy nuggets' out of my bag. I called them on many occasions and picked their brains –asking questions about the steps I should take during my transition.

Now grant it, they did not know they were mentoring me and pushing me. I have seen them both do amazing things. Ironically, they are both DJs – no relevance to this conversation but that thought just popped in my head – They have an achievement mindset they pass on to anyone that is willing to listen. They are 'happy nugget grabbers'.

I have thanked Sean and Tony countless times but I am sure they will be somewhat surprised when they read this book; after they buy it of course. No one really knows the impact they have on someone else's life. When you look at your boss, what impact does it have? Does it motivate you to want to do something better or do you see yourself filling their corporate shoes?

Mama: Yea, I am going there -in a word, Mama! – My mother has a crazy work ethic – When she wants something she does it – When she needs something she gets it. I would never hear the end of it if I do not give her credit for my work ethic. She definitely gave me my passion for reading.

Just Do the Work! –I am now blessed to be around a bunch of over achievers – I associate with over achievers. Just about everyone I know is working on improvement – Looking to do better! They have the rehabilitation of career mindset - They realize learning and perfecting doesn't stop. The difference between them and you – They are 'do-doing' it! Everyone once in a while, I have to reach my hand in their 'happy nugget' bag and they do the same for me.

I found that as I raised my bar – some folk thought I was lowering them. It was not about them, it was about me! I kept pushing – Remember when we started this journey I told you the goal is to not just have you walk but to have you run – To put you in the position to give back! You have to make this personal – You have to get it in your mind that you can accomplish anything 'You' put before you–and you will become who you say you want to be.

You have made a declaration! You have looked at your boss! You have looked at Yourself! You are ready for a change! You know your 'range of motion'. You are building Your strength – Now, Let's put it all together –STOP!!!

O. K.! Let's address the excuses! – I apologize in advance because the excuse chapter will be extremely short. It is time to loose your grip on your happy nugget bag!

It is time to turn it over and empty it out!
It is time to say it's about you!
It's time to say 'You Will!"
It's Your Time!
You Can!

The Declaration:

"I do not like my current position and I am committed to making a change! I have looked at my boss and I do/do not want to be in that position. I know I have to make a change and my first step is to "Determine my Range of Motion" – my second step is to "Build up my Strength" – The final step is to Put it All Together!"

Questions:

Do you believe it is ok for the 'Duh Saints' to do nothing to progress their career? Now we know 'He is Able" –But what is our responsibility?

_____

_____

_____

_____

Who told you that you can't succeed?

_____

_____

_____

_____

Where did you receive the mentality it is ok to be unhappy with your job?

_____

_____

_____

_____

_____

List three of your most commonly used "Happy Nuggets" – What scriptures do you use to justify where you are in life? Based on your self-admitted unhappiness?

1._____

2._____

3._____

Notes

_____

_____

_____

_____

_____

_____

_____

_____

_____

_____

_____

_____

_____

_____

Listen – You have to stop talking about it, and do it. You have to want it more than the people telling you to get it.

Proverbs 14:23 ESV

In all toil there is profit, but mere talk tends only to poverty.

1 Corinthians 10:31 ESV

So, whether you eat or drink, or whatever you do, do all to the glory of God.

Proverbs 6:6-8 ESV

Go to the ant, O sluggard; consider her ways, and be wise. Without having any chief, officer, or ruler, she prepares her bread in summer and gathers her food in harvest.

Chapter 8 ➤

What's Your Excuses Now?

"the short chapter"

By now you know the only excuse you can have is you. Do we need to recite the declaration again?

> *I do not like my current position and I am committed to making a change! I have looked at my boss and I do/do not want to be in that position. I know I have to make a change and my first step is to "Determine my Range of Motion" – my second step is to "Build up my Strength" – The final step is to...*

Before you get to the final step, you need to lighten the load. You need to work on emptying your bag of 'happy nuggets'. One of the goals of this book was to be short. Procrastinators Don't Read! You won't read a long book! After the 2nd chapter you would have shut the book and put it in your 'happy nugget bag' – Someone is going to ask you what you been up to – You are going to stick out your chest – stand up straight and say I just finished 'Look at Your Boss' – I am rehabilitating my career. Then you will put the thought and the book back in the bag; the 'happy nugget' bag is full again. If we spent an entire chapter on excuses you and I would be here for hours; wasting time. You did that enough! STOP!!! You need to decide is this book a 'happy nugget' or Motivation?

Just take the declaration, you can move on:

I do not like my current position and I am committed to making a change! I have looked at my boss and I do/do not want to be in that position. I know I have to make a change and my first step is to "Determine my Range of Motion" – my second step is to "Build up my Strength" – The final step is to Put it All Together!

Questions:

Is there really any excuse not to work on becoming better if you are not happy?

_____

_____

_____

_____

Take your list of 'Happy Nuggets" from the previous 7 chapters, list the seven you can throw out now.

1. _____

2. _____

3. _____

4. _____

5. _____

6. _____

7. _____

You have about 14 to go – Throw out 6 more.

1. _____

2. _____

3. _____

4. _____

5. _____

6. _____

13 is an unlucky number so throw out 3more – List the 5 remaining – What will you need to do to get rid of the last 5 'Happy Nugget' so you can move on.

1. _____

2. _____

3. _____

4. _____

5. _____

Notes

_____

_____

_____

_____

_____

_____

_____

_____

_____

_____

_____

_____

_____

_____

_____

_____

_____

_____

_____

Look at Your boss!

Chapter 9 ➤

Putting It All Together!

"Shhhhh, It's time"

I promise I am not going to spend the next 5 pages recapping and talking about the entire process we have talked about already – If the truth be

> *You are Ready! – You are Willing! – You are Able!*

told, we could have completed this entire book in one page – I showed you the example when we started . See the page before Chapter 1. You need to make moves! You need to do something. You need to do a check-up from the neck-up. Here is the process:

1. Look at your boss! Look at Yourself!
2. Make a declaration!
3. Grab your bag of "Happy Nuggets" and toss it out the window!
4. Open the window!
5. What do you do-do? Research, plan, and take action!
6. There are no acceptable excuses.
7. If you are still not convinced you can do it – email me!
8. It's time to get personal!
9. You and me "mano-a-mano"-

Now if you are feeling short changed – and you need more information – hmu - If you need my hand in your 'happy nugget' bag hmu.

I knew a Career Counselor that had a mantra and a sign in her office that read, 'I do not do pity parties' –I adopted that mantra so Please understand "I do not do pity parties'

You have to take action – stop talking about it and be about it - I really wanted you to finish reading this book and be inspired! You did it! You reached another milestone – Take this new found confidence and make a plan. You are Ready! – You are Willing! – You are Able! – Listen, we are regular folk that need to look at our boss, look at our self, and then rehabilitate our career!

Well, we have reached the end of the road. The beginning for you. The cool thing is thanks to 'social media' this is not the end of this book. You can reach out to me directly; as often as possible. The rest of the nuggets are free. You will be able to reach me via Facebook, Twitter, website, and listen to my radio blog! I will provide you with career updates and tips from industry experts. Most importantly – I will never give up on 'You' or you.

Contact Me Now:

http://www.facebook.com/LookatyourBoss
Tweet @lookatyourboss

The Declaration:

"I do not like my current position and I am committed to making a change! I have looked at my boss and I do/do not want to be in that position. I know I have to make a change and my first step is to "Determine my Range of Motion" – my second step is to "Build up my Strength" – The final step is to Put it All Together!"

Notes

_____

_____

_____

_____

_____

_____

_____

_____

_____

_____

Listen, you are the only person in a position to decide what you want and then make it happen. If you're not putting forth the effort to change you will always work in a job you don't want.

Proverbs 12:24 ESV

The hand of the diligent will rule, while the slothful will be put to forced labor.

1 Thessalonians 4:11-12 ESV

And to aspire to live quietly, and to mind your own affairs, and to work with your hands, as we instructed you, so that you may walk properly before outsiders and be dependent on no one.

Jeremiah 29:11 ESV

For I know the plans I have for you, declares the Lord, plans for welfare and not for evil, to give you a future and a hope.

Chapter 10 ➤

The Excuse Chapter

Excuse in a word: You!

The Declaration:

I do not like my current position and I am committed to making a change! I have looked at my boss and I do/do not want to be like that. I know I have to make a change and my first step is to "Determine my Range of Motion" – my second step is to "Build up my Strength" – The final step is to Put it All Together!

Put it together!

Epilogue

Look at your Boss

Rehabilitation for your Career

a. Sit down for five minutes... (a minute if you are on the clock) Look at your boss!
b. Is this a position you want to have?
c. Is this a position you do not want to have?

Once you answer those questions – after you take a hard look at your boss does for a living. If this is not something you want to do – You need to make a change. If this is something you want to do, you need to make a change; either way it requires you take a look at your boss, take a look at yourself, and then make a change. You must do something. It requires **You** to take action.

The End

Really it's that simple!

Notes

Made in the USA
Charleston, SC
06 January 2013